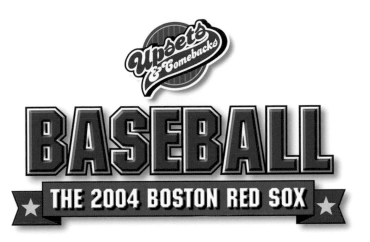

BASEBALL
THE 2004 BOSTON RED SOX

by **Michael Sandler**

Consultant: Jim Sherman
Head Baseball Coach
University of Delaware

BEARPORT
PUBLISHING COMPANY, INC.

New York, New York

Credits

Editorial development by Judy Nayer

Cover and title page, ©Mike Blake/Reuters/Corbis; Pages 4-5 (both), AP/Wide World Photos; 6, ©JESSICA RINALDI/Reuters/Corbis; 7, AP/Wide World Photos; 8 (both), AP/Wide World Photos; 9 (top), FPG/Getty Images; 9 (bottom), National Baseball Hall of Fame Library/MLB Photos via Getty Images; 10, Focus on Sport/Getty Images; 11, George Tiedemann/Sports Illustrated; 12-13, ©Bettmann/CORBIS; 13, Bruce Bennett Studios/Getty Images; 14, ©Shaun Best/Reuters/Corbis; 15, ©Henny Abrams/Stringer/Reuters/Corbis; 16, National Baseball Hall of Fame Library/MLB Photos via Getty Images; 17, AP/Wide World Photos; 18, Damian Strohmeyer/Sports Illustrated; 19, Robert Beck/Sports Illustrated; 20, Rich Pilling/MLB Photos via Getty Images; 21, ©Shaun Best/Reuters/Corbis; 22, Ezra Shaw/Getty Images; 23, ©SHAUN BEST/Reuters/Corbis; 24, ©Mike Blake/Reuters/Corbis; 25, Al Bello/Getty Images; 26, Elsa/Getty Images; 27, AP/Wide World Photos.

Design and production by
Ralph Cosentino

Library of Congress Cataloging-in-Publication Data

Sandler, Michael.
  Baseball : the 2004 Boston Red Sox / by Michael Sandler.
     p. cm. — (Upsets & comebacks)
  Includes bibliographical references and index.
  ISBN 1-59716-165-9 (library binding) — ISBN 1-59716-191-8 (pbk.)
 1. Boston Red Sox (Baseball Team)—History—Juvenile literature. 2. Baseball—Massachusetts—Boston—History—Juvenile literature. 3. World Series (Baseball) 2004—Juvenile literature. I. Title. II. Series.

  GV875.B62S26 2006
  796.357'64'0974461—dc22

                         2005026090

For more information, write to Bearport Publishing Company, Inc., 101 Fifth Avenue, Suite 6R, New York, New York 10003. Printed in the United States of America.

1 2 3 4 5 6 7 8 9 10

Table of Contents

Not Again!

It was the bottom of the ninth inning. Boston Red Sox fans squirmed in their seats. Their team had only one more chance at bat. Time was running out.

If the Red Sox didn't score, it meant another season without going to the **World Series**. It meant the New York Yankees would play in the World Series instead of the Red Sox.

The Red Sox were facing the Yankees' best pitcher, Mariano "Mr. Automatic" Rivera. Getting outs was usually "automatic" for Mariano.

The Red Sox fans hated losing, but they were used to it. **Rooting** for the Red Sox meant rooting for a losing team. Their team hadn't won a **championship** in 86 years!

Only people over 90 years old could remember the last time the Red Sox won a World Series! Fans young and old, however, still rooted for the team.

A baseball game has nine innings. Each inning has two parts, a top and a bottom. The visiting team bats in the top of the inning. The home team bats in the bottom. Each team gets three outs per inning.

The World Series

The World Series is held each October. Only two of baseball's 30 **major league** teams get to play in it. One team is the American League (AL) champion. The other is the National League (NL) champion. Getting to the World Series and winning it are the **ultimate** goals for any baseball team.

Fans view World Series items.

In 2004, the Red Sox and the Yankees were playing each other for the American League Championship. The first team to win four games would move on to the World Series.

The Yankees had won the first three games. The Red Sox were just one loss from ending their season.

The first World Series trophy was awarded in 1967 to the St. Louis Cardinals. A new trophy is created each year. Here New York Yankees manager Joe Torre holds the team's World Series trophy in 1998.

Baseball uses a "best-of-seven" playoff to decide the winner of both the league championships and the World Series. Two teams play against each other until one team wins four games. The series can last up to seven games.

The History of the Red Sox

The Red Sox are one of baseball's oldest teams. They began playing over a century ago. In the team's early days, winning was rarely a problem.

Boston won the very first World Series. They **defeated** the Pittsburgh Pirates back in 1903. Then they won again in 1912, 1915, 1916, and 1918.

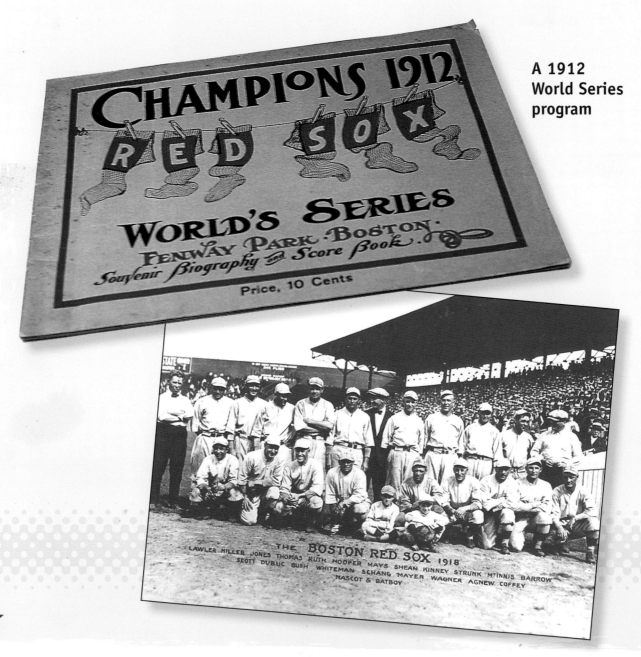

A 1912 World Series program

Red Sox fans in Fenway Park, Boston's home field, at the start of the 1912 World Series

Each season began with big plans and high hopes. The Red Sox always had hitters who could slam **home runs**, and pitchers who could hurl **strikes**. Each season, Boston seemed to win another pennant or league championship. The flagpoles at Fenway Park were crowded with pennant flags.

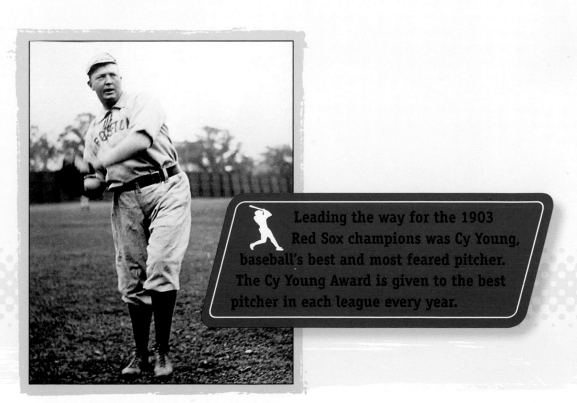

Leading the way for the 1903 Red Sox champions was Cy Young, baseball's best and most feared pitcher. The Cy Young Award is given to the best pitcher in each league every year.

After 1918, however, everything went wrong. Whenever Boston had a chance to win a World Series, they let it slip away.

This bad luck followed them to Game 6 in the 1986 World Series. Boston was playing the New York Mets. They were ahead by one run, and just a single pitch away from victory. If pitcher Bob Stanley could throw one more strike, Boston would win the series!

Bob Stanley gets ready to throw a pitch.

Instead, Stanley threw a **wild pitch**, and a
Mets **runner** scored to tie the game. Next, Boston
infielder Bill Buckner let a ball roll between his legs.
Another Met scored, giving New York the victory.

Ray Knight scored the winning run for the Mets.

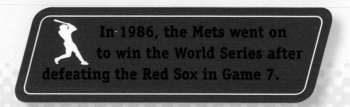

In 1986, the Mets went on
to win the World Series after
defeating the Red Sox in Game 7.

One team that caused the Red Sox a lot of grief was the St. Louis Cardinals. Twice, the two teams met in the World Series.

In 1946, Boston was expected to win easily. However, the series went all the way to seven games. The Red Sox faced the Cardinals at home in Fenway Park. Crowds of Red Sox fans were ready to cheer if Boston won. Instead, they left the stadium silently. The Cardinals won 4–3.

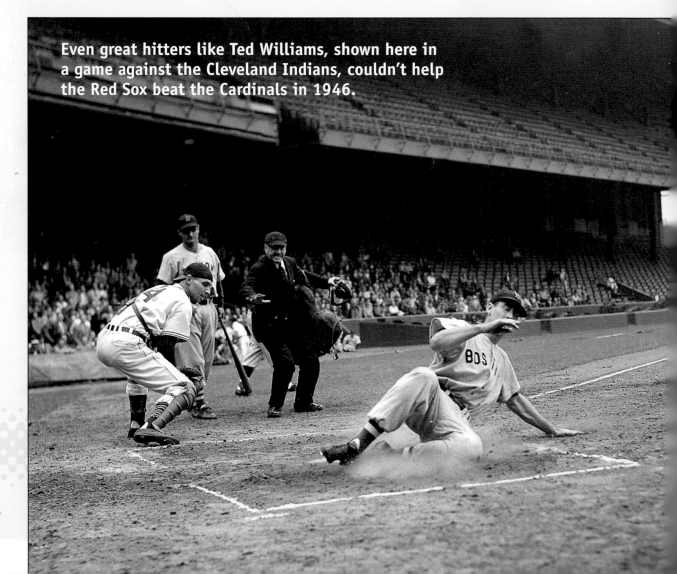

Even great hitters like Ted Williams, shown here in a game against the Cleveland Indians, couldn't help the Red Sox beat the Cardinals in 1946.

In 1967, the series also went to a seventh game. Older fans remembered the 1946 loss. They hoped this game would end differently. However, it didn't. As the Cardinals celebrated, Boston fans walked out silently again.

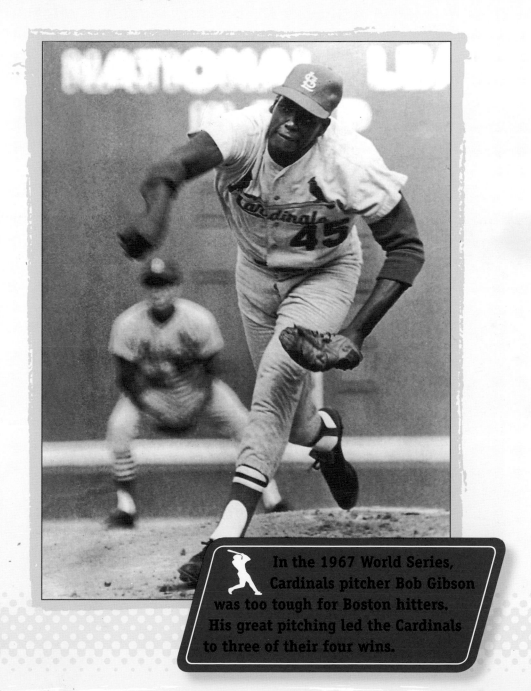

In the 1967 World Series, Cardinals pitcher Bob Gibson was too tough for Boston hitters. His great pitching led the Cardinals to three of their four wins.

Most of the time, however, Boston didn't even get to the World Series. The New York Yankees were always in their way.

The Yankees were Boston's biggest **rival**. Both teams were in the American League. Since only one AL team could be in the series, the Red Sox couldn't go if the Yankees made it. It seemed like the Yankees almost always won, often after beating Boston in a playoff series.

New York Yankees Derek Jeter hits a home run in Game 3 of the 2003 American League Championship Series.

From 1996 to 2003, the Yankees made it to the World Series six times. Boston didn't make it at all.

Boston pitcher Tim Wakefield walks off the field after giving up the game-winning home run to the New York Yankees, who would advance to the 2003 World Series.

When a game is tied at the end of nine innings, both teams get to bat in an extra inning. The game continues until the tie is broken. In 2003, the Yankees broke the hearts of Red Sox fans by winning playoff Game 7 with an 11th-inning home run.

Some people said the Red Sox couldn't win because of a curse on the team! Losing was Boston's punishment for trading away a player named Babe Ruth.

Back in the days when Boston was still winning, Babe Ruth was their finest player. The Babe was the most powerful **slugger** baseball has ever known. The ball shot off his bat like a rocket. He hit home runs by the handful—two, even three in a game!

Babe Ruth started out as a pitcher, but he hit the ball so hard he became a hitter instead.

The Babe helped Boston win three championships.
Then, in 1920, the Red Sox sold him—to the Yankees.
Right about then Boston began to lose.

After getting
Babe Ruth, the
Yankees won 26
championships.
After losing him,
the Red Sox
didn't win any
championships.

In 1927, Babe Ruth hit
a record 60 home runs
for the Yankees. The record
lasted for over 30 years.

The 2004 Season

Sometimes at a season's end, Red Sox fans **vowed** never to watch another game. By **opening day**, however, the fans always changed their minds. They loved their team too much—win or lose—to stay away.

During the 2004 season, the fans were back to cheer for the Red Sox. They cheered every home run Manny Ramirez slammed. They cheered every blazing strike Pedro Martinez threw. They cheered every diving catch Johnny Damon made.

Manny Ramirez hitting a home run

They cheered when Boston reached the American League Championship Series against the Yankees— though they fully expected to lose.

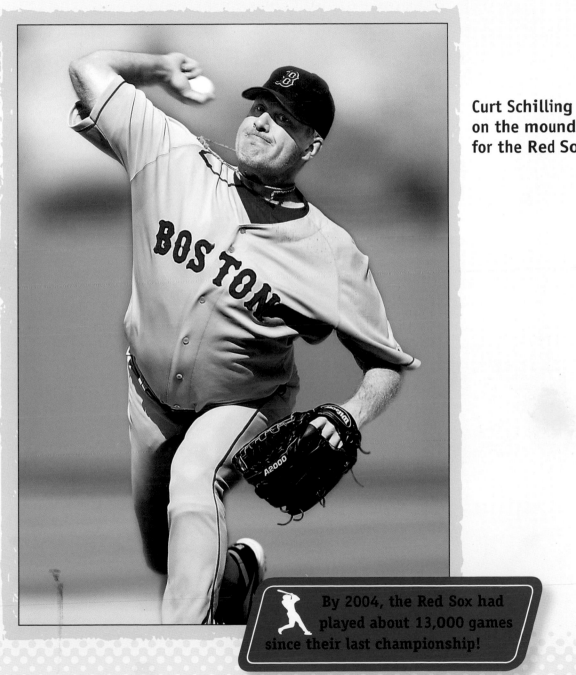

Curt Schilling on the mound for the Red Sox

By 2004, the Red Sox had played about 13,000 games since their last championship!

Staying Alive

Fans weren't surprised when the Yankees won the first three games. They weren't surprised when Boston faced **elimination** in the ninth inning of Game 4. History said that Boston always lost. However, this time they didn't.

Getting outs usually came easily for Yankees pitcher Mariano Rivera, but he **walked** a Boston batter. Then Bill Mueller slapped a **single**. A player already on base came home to score. The game was tied!

Bill Mueller hits the game-tying single.

The game went into extra innings. In the bottom of the 12th, with a runner on base, David Ortiz smashed a home run. Two runs scored. The Red Sox won, 6–4. The season, however, wasn't over yet!

David Ortiz hits the game-winning home run.

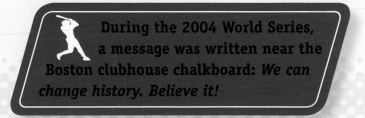

During the 2004 World Series, a message was written near the Boston clubhouse chalkboard: *We can change history. Believe it!*

Bye-Bye, Yankees!

The Red Sox were still behind three games to one. To beat the Yankees, they needed to win three games in a row. Comebacks like this only happened in players' dreams. They didn't happen in real life.

This time, however, their dreams kept coming true. In Game 5, David Ortiz was the hero again! His single in the 14th inning brought in the winning run. In Game 6, Curt Schilling pitched incredibly to give Boston the win. In Game 7, the Red Sox smashed in ten runs against Yankees pitchers.

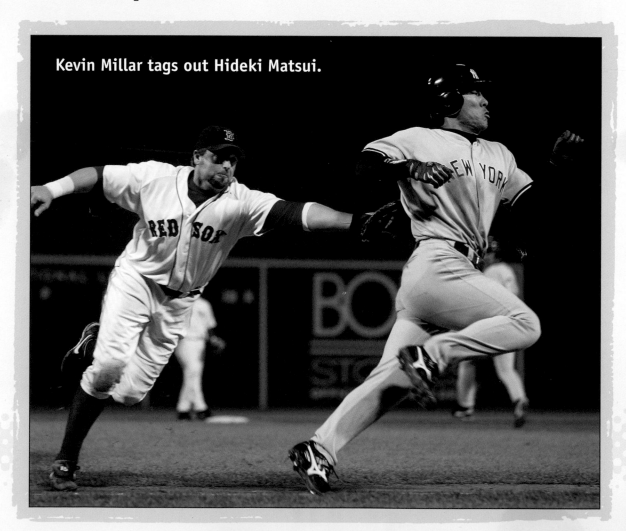

Kevin Millar tags out Hideki Matsui.

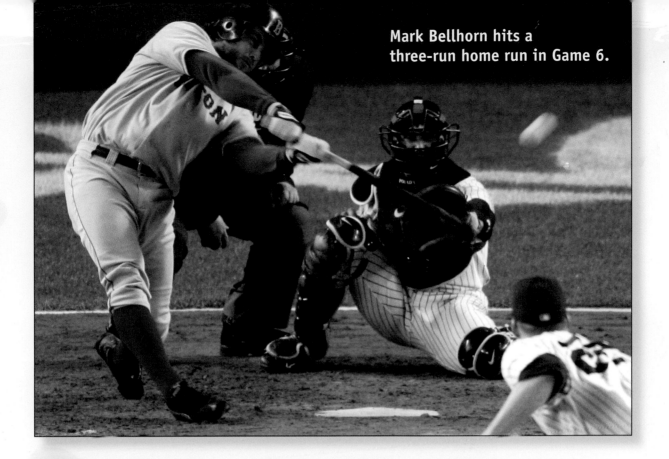

Mark Bellhorn hits a
three-run home run in Game 6.

The Red Sox had changed history. They had beaten
the Yankees. They were going to the World Series!

★ THE 2004 AMERICAN LEAGUE CHAMPIONSHIP SERIES ★

Game 1	Yankees 10, Red Sox 7	Game 4	Red Sox 6, Yankees 4
Game 2	Yankees 3, Red Sox 1	Game 5	Red Sox 5, Yankees 4
Game 3	Yankees 19, Red Sox 8	Game 6	Red Sox 4, Yankees 2
★ ★ ★ ★ ★ ★ ★ ★		Game 7	Red Sox 10, Yankees 3

The Red Sox comeback
was the greatest in baseball
history. No team had ever come
back to win a series after losing
the first three games.

Hello, Cardinals!

Boston's job wasn't done. To break the 86-year-old curse, they still had to beat the National League champion. The team was another old enemy, the St. Louis Cardinals!

In 2004, the Cardinals had won 105 games, more than any other team. They had a **lineup** filled with sluggers. Pitchers hated to throw against them, fearing the shower of home runs.

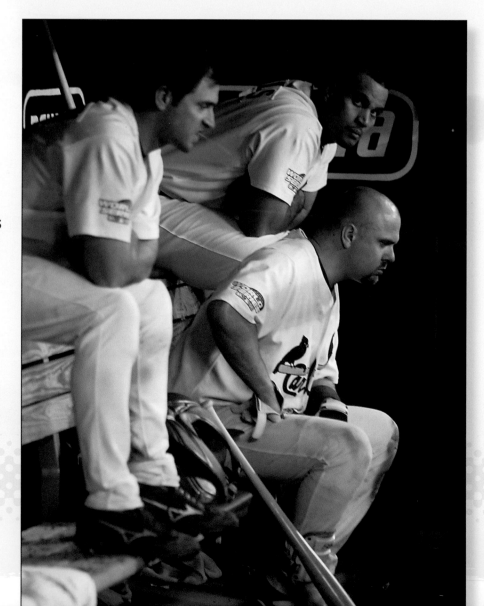

Even big St. Louis hitters, like Larry Walker (middle), couldn't hit Boston's pitches.

Somehow, Red Sox pitchers kept the Cardinals from scoring. Boston took the lead in the very first inning of the very first game. They never looked back. Boston won the series in four straight games.

The Boston Red Sox celebrate their first World Series win in 86 years.

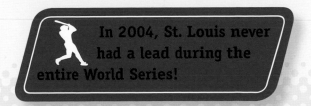

In 2004, St. Louis never had a lead during the entire World Series!

★ The Curse Is Over! ★

Finally, all the pain was forgotten. All the losses were washed away. For both players and fans, the past no longer mattered.

The Red Sox players ran out onto the field. They met at home plate, jumping up-and-down, screaming, and hugging one another. Some of the players were crying tears of joy.

Boston fans cheer during the Red Sox World Series Championship parade.

Boston fans in the stadium went crazy. Boston fans at home leaned out their windows and yelled for joy. Except for the very oldest fans—those who could still remember 1918—winning was a brand-new experience. Their team, the Boston Red Sox, was baseball's champion!

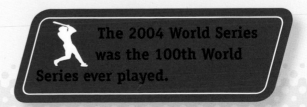

The 2004 World Series was the 100th World Series ever played.

Just the Facts

More About the Red Sox and the World Series

★ **Traveling Trophy**—It had been so long since Boston had won a trophy that people wanted to see what it looked like. The Red Sox sent the trophy on a tour. It journeyed across Massachusetts for months, visiting 351 cities and towns.

★ **Moon Magic**—Was it the moon that changed Boston's luck? The night the Red Sox won the 2004 World Series, a total lunar eclipse was visible. This was the only time such an eclipse had happened during a World Series game. In a lunar eclipse, you can't see the moon because it is covered by Earth's shadow.

Timeline
This timeline shows some important events in the history of the Boston Red Sox.

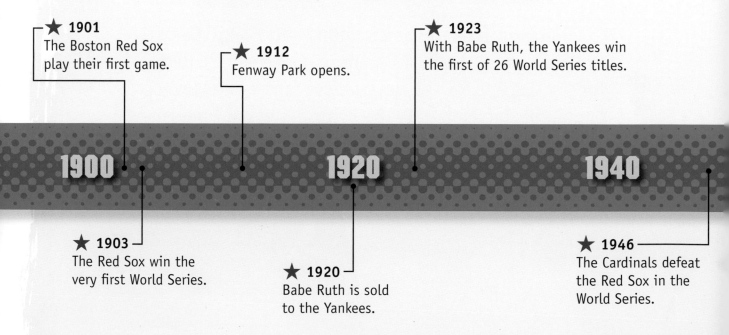

★ **1901**
The Boston Red Sox play their first game.

★ **1912**
Fenway Park opens.

★ **1923**
With Babe Ruth, the Yankees win the first of 26 World Series titles.

1900

1920

1940

★ **1903**
The Red Sox win the very first World Series.

★ **1920**
Babe Ruth is sold to the Yankees.

★ **1946**
The Cardinals defeat the Red Sox in the World Series.

★ **The Babe**—Babe Ruth was worth much more than the $100,000 Boston got when they traded him to the Yankees. How good was he?

• Hit 714 home runs during his career

• The only player ever to hit three home runs in a World Series game on two different occasions

• Led the American League in home runs 12 times

• Often hit more home runs each year with the Yankees than all 25 players on the Red Sox team combined

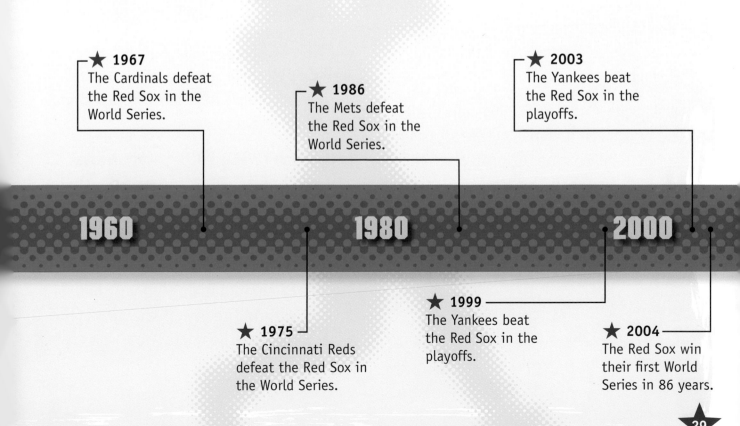

★ **1967**
The Cardinals defeat the Red Sox in the World Series.

★ **1986**
The Mets defeat the Red Sox in the World Series.

★ **2003**
The Yankees beat the Red Sox in the playoffs.

1960

1980

2000

★ **1975**
The Cincinnati Reds defeat the Red Sox in the World Series.

★ **1999**
The Yankees beat the Red Sox in the playoffs.

★ **2004**
The Red Sox win their first World Series in 86 years.

Glossary

championship (CHAM-pee-uhn-*ship*) a contest or final game of a series that decides which team will be the winner

defeated (di-FEE-tid) beat

elimination (uh-*lim*-uh-NAY-shun) to be removed from a contest because a person lost

home runs (HOHM RUHNZ) hits that allow the batter to run around all the bases and score

infielder (IN-feeld-ur) a person who plays a position in the infield, which is made up of first base, second base, third base, or shortstop

lineup (LINE-uhp) the group of players, in a specific order, who come to bat for a baseball team

major league (MAY-jur LEEG) either of the two main groups, American League or National League, of professional baseball teams in the United States

opening day (OHP-en-ing DAY) a team's first game of a new baseball season

playoff (PLAY-awf) final games to decide which teams will play in a championship

rival (RYE-vuhl) a player or team one is always trying to beat

rooting (ROOT-ing) cheering

runner (RUN-ur) one who runs the bases

single (SING-guhl) a hit that allows the batter to go to first base safely

slugger (SLUHG-er) a player who can hit the ball hard and far

strikes (STRIKES) pitches that pass over the plate between a batter's chest and knees; or pitches that the batter swings at and misses; or pitches that the batter swings at and hits foul with less than two strikes

ultimate (UHL-tuh-mit) greatest or best

vowed (VOWD) promised oneself something

walked (WALKT) put a batter at first base by throwing four pitches that aren't strikes

wild pitch (WILD PICH) a pitch that is so high, low, or to the side, that a catcher can't grab it; allows a runner to advance at least one base

World Series (WURLD SIHR-eez) the yearly championship playoff between the winning teams of the two major U.S. baseball leagues

Bibliography

The *Boston Globe's* Red Sox Championship Commemorative Section www.boston.com/sports/baseball/redsox/articles/2004/10/31/commemorative/

Montville, Leigh. *Why Not Us?* New York: PublicAffairs (2004).

Robbins, Mike, ed. *The Yankees vs. Red Sox Reader.* New York: Carroll & Graf (2005).

Vaccaro, Mike. *Emperors and Idiots.* New York: Doubleday (2005).

Read More

Burleigh, Robert. *Home Run: The Story of Babe Ruth.* New York: Silver Whistle (1998).

Shaughnessy, Dan. *The Legend of the Curse of the Bambino.* New York: Simon & Schuster (2005).

Sheldon, Heather Barlow. *Seymour's Soaring Red Sox: A Bird's Eye View of the 2004 World Series.* Acton, MA: Cassiopeia Press (2005).

Tavares, Matt. *Zachary's Ball.* Cambridge, MA: Candlewick Press (2000).

Learn More Online

Visit these Web sites to learn more about baseball, the Boston Red Sox, and the World Series:

www.exploratorium.edu/baseball

www.worldseries.com

Index

About the Author

Michael Sandler lives in Brooklyn, New York. He has written numerous books on sports for children and young adults. His two children, Laszlo and Asha, are not quite old enough to read them yet.